HIP-HOP

50 Cent

Ashanti

Beyoncé

Mary J. Blige

Chris Brown

Mariah Carey

Sean "Diddy" Combs

Dr. Dre

Missy Elliott

Eminem

Hip-Hop: A Short History

Jay-Z

Alicia Keys

LL Cool J

Ludacris

Nelly

Notorious B.I.G.

Queen Latifah

Reverend Run (Run-D.M.C.)

Will Smith

Snoop Dogg

Tupac

Usher

Kanye West

Pharrell Williams

Mariah Carey

Celicia Scott

Mason Crest Publishers

Mariah Carey

FRONTIS Mariah Carey's personal and professional lives have been up and down, but she's definitely on top of both now!

PRODUCED BY 21ST CENTURY PUBLISHING AND COMMUNICATIONS, INC.

EDITORIAL BY HARDING HOUSE PUBLISHING SERVICES, INC.

MASON CREST PUBLISHERS INC.
370 Reed Road
Broomall, Pennsylvania 19008
(866)MCP-BOOK (toll free)
www.masoncrest.com

Printed in the U.S.A.

First Printing

9 8 7 6 5 4 3 2 1

Library of Congress Cataloging-in-Publication Data

Scott, Celicia.
   Mariah Carey / by Celicia Scott.
      p. cm. — (Hip-hop)
Hardback edition: ISBN-13: 978-1-4222-0114-5
Hardback edition: ISBN-10: 1-4222-0114-7
Paperback edition: ISBN-13: 978-1-4222-0265-4
   1. Carey, Mariah—Juvenile literature. 2. Singers—United States—Biography—
Juvenile literature. I. Title. II. Series.
ML3930.C257S36 2007
782.42164092—dc22   2006008650

Contents

Hip-Hop Timeline

1974 Hip-hop pioneer Afrika Bambaataa organizes the Universal Zulu Nation.

1988 *Yo! MTV Raps* premieres on MTV.

1970s Hip-hop as a cultural movement begins in the Bronx, New York City.

1985 *Krush Groove*, a hip-hop film about Def Jam Recordings, is released featuring Run-D.M.C., Kurtis Blow, LL Cool J, and the Beastie Boys.

1970s DJ Kool Herc pioneers the use of breaks, isolations, and repeats using two turntables.

1979 The Sugarhill Gang's song "Rapper's Delight" is the first hip-hop single to go gold.

1986 Run-D.M.C. are the first rappers to appear on the cover of *Rolling Stone* magazine.

1970   1980   1988

1976 Grandmaster Flash & the Furious Five pioneer hip-hop MCing and freestyle battles.

1986 Beastie Boys' album *Licensed to Ill* is released and becomes the best-selling rap album of the 1980s.

1970s Break dancing emerges at parties and in public places in New York City.

1982 Afrika Bambaataa embarks on the first European hip-hop tour.

1970s Graffiti artist Vic pioneers tagging on subway trains in New York City.

1988 Hip-hop music annual record sales reaches $100 million.

1984 *Graffiti Rock*, the first hip-hop television program, premieres.

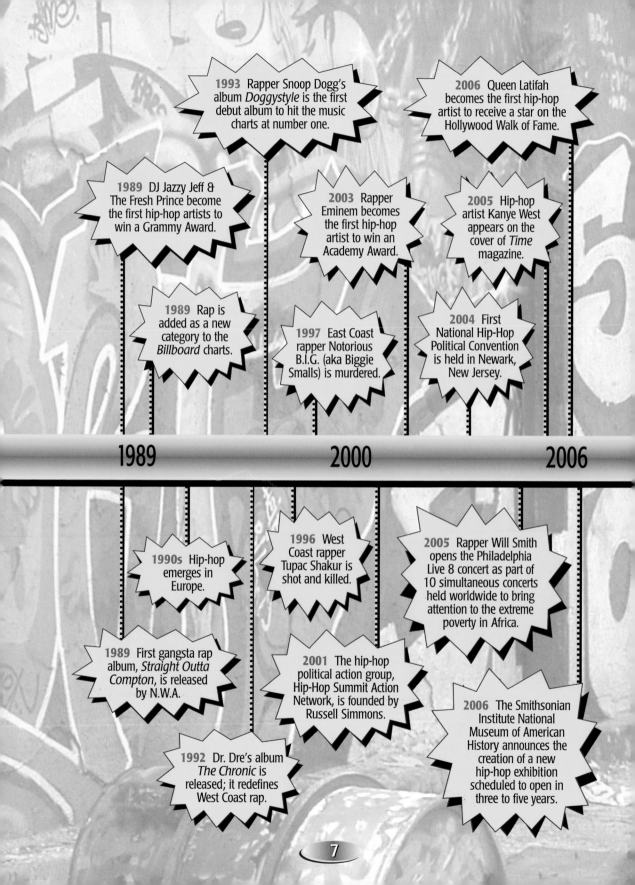

1993 Rapper Snoop Dogg's album *Doggystyle* is the first debut album to hit the music charts at number one.

2006 Queen Latifah becomes the first hip-hop artist to receive a star on the Hollywood Walk of Fame.

1989 DJ Jazzy Jeff & The Fresh Prince become the first hip-hop artists to win a Grammy Award.

2003 Rapper Eminem becomes the first hip-hop artist to win an Academy Award.

2005 Hip-hop artist Kanye West appears on the cover of *Time* magazine.

1989 Rap is added as a new category to the *Billboard* charts.

1997 East Coast rapper Notorious B.I.G. (aka Biggie Smalls) is murdered.

2004 First National Hip-Hop Political Convention is held in Newark, New Jersey.

1989

2000

2006

1990s Hip-hop emerges in Europe.

1996 West Coast rapper Tupac Shakur is shot and killed.

2005 Rapper Will Smith opens the Philadelphia Live 8 concert as part of 10 simultaneous concerts held worldwide to bring attention to the extreme poverty in Africa.

1989 First gangsta rap album, *Straight Outta Compton*, is released by N.W.A.

2001 The hip-hop political action group, Hip-Hop Summit Action Network, is founded by Russell Simmons.

1992 Dr. Dre's album *The Chronic* is released; it redefines West Coast rap.

2006 The Smithsonian Institute National Museum of American History announces the creation of a new hip-hop exhibition scheduled to open in three to five years.

In July 2005, Mariah Carey lent her five-octave voice to the fight against poverty in Africa as one of the featured performers at the Live 8 Concert in London. Once again, Mariah was on top of the music world.

1

The View from the Top

On July 2, 2005, the Live 8 Concert took place on stages around the globe. The musical extravaganza was an effort to pressure the world's eight major **industrialized** nations into working harder to fight poverty, especially in Africa. The biggest stars in the music world took part in the concert—including Mariah Carey.

Mariah performed at the Live 8 Concert in London's Hyde Park. Her incredible five-octave voice soared out over the audience on behalf of the world's poorest people. In a way, her voice was her prayer.

Music had always been Mariah's prayer, right from the beginning. In 2005, as she performed for Live 8, she was at the top of her career, in a place where her music had power to change the world. This had always been her dream. In June 2005, she had told *Parade* magazine that music "was a prayer that I prayed with my whole heart. It was something I truly believed would happen, and it did."

Looking Back

In the late 1950s, Patricia Hickey, the daughter of Irish immigrants, was singing for the **prestigious** New York City Opera. Meanwhile, Alfred Roy Carey, the son of black immigrants from Venezuela, had studied math and science in college and became an aeronautical engineer. They met, fell in love, and married in 1960.

"My parents had a lot of strikes against them just being an **interracial** couple," Mariah later told *Jet* magazine. "There was a lot of racism in the sixties and seventies. My brother and sister and I were the products of forbidden love."

In 1960, the **civil rights movement** was just getting off the ground. Schools, restaurants, and other public buildings were still strictly **segregated** in many areas of the country. In many cases, black-and-white marriages were not accepted by either African Americans or whites, and Patricia and Alfred had to face the challenge of **bigotry**. Mariah told Oprah Winfrey years later:

> **"From the start, my mother's family basically disowned her when she married my father. . . . All sorts of crazy things happened. Their car got blown up, and their dogs were poisoned. . . . When they moved to an all-white neighborhood, my mother had to buy the house because the owners would not sell if they knew she had a black husband."**

Once, while they sat eating dinner, a bullet burst through the window, just missing them both. The constant stress "put a strain on their relationship that would never quit," Mariah told *People* magazine. "There was always this tension, and they just fought all the time."

Early in the marriage, Mariah's older brother Morgan and her sister Allison were born. The family moved back and forth between New York City and Rhode Island. By the late 1960s, Patricia had reestablished her musical career (after stopping for a few years when her children were babies), and she was first soloist at the New York City Opera. And then, to her surprise, she found out she was pregnant again.

Mariah was born on March 27, 1970. She was named after the song "They Call the Wind Maria" from the Broadway musical *Paint Your Wagon*.

Music would always be at the center of Mariah's life. By the time she was two years old, she could hear any note and sing it back exactly.

As a biracial teen, Mariah faced obstacles and feelings many other teens do not. In 1999, Mariah and her mother appeared on the *Oprah Winfrey Show* to share her experiences with other biracial children. This is just one way Mariah tries to make a difference.

"Every song that came on the radio, T.V. commercials, I would just sing along with anything I heard," Mariah told *People*.

Mariah grew up knowing that she and her family were different from other people in their mostly white neighborhood. She told *Eva* magazine, "My brother was always getting beaten up. My sister Allison always got picked on because she had the darkest skin."

Growing Up

In 1973, when Mariah was three years old, the stress became too much for her parents, and they divorced. Mariah and her brother Morgan lived with their mother, while Allison moved out with their father. Patricia became a single parent, struggling to care for her children between her responsibilities as a singer. She often brought her youngest daughter with her, so Mariah became comfortable around adults—and she soaked up their music like a sponge.

When Mariah was four, her mother began her daughter's formal voice lessons. Mariah told the *New York Times*, "My mom always told me 'You are special. You have talent.' From a very early age, she gave me the belief that I could do this."

During Mariah's growing-up years, she was exposed to many kinds of music. She learned about opera and folk music from her mother; her older brother and sister taught her about **soul** and **R&B**; and her grandmother taught her to appreciate **gospel**. But Mariah's favorite singer was Minnie Riperton, a soul singer who had a five-to-seven octave range. Mariah listened to Riperton's records and did her best to imitate her.

Mariah was obsessed with music. "My mother would have to tear me away from the radio every night just to get me to go to bed," she told *Modern Woman* magazine. "But then I would sneak back down to the kitchen, bring the radio back to my bedroom, and listen to it under the covers. I used to sing myself to sleep every night."

In many ways, music was Mariah's only friend. Since her mother often worked three jobs to make ends meet, Mariah did not always get the attention and security she craved. The family moved around a lot, which meant that Mariah seldom had a chance to make friends or gain a sense of security from familiar surroundings.

Learning Life's Lessons

With her mother's uncertain lifestyle, Mariah's growing-up years were not as safe and sheltered as most middle-class girls her age. Her sister Allison got pregnant when she was sixteen, and many of the people around Mariah made choices that led them into trouble of various kinds. But Mariah was determined to learn from others' mistakes; she had big plans for her life, and she did not want to jeopardize them.

Whenever Mariah felt discouraged, she would burst into song (whether she was alone or in public didn't matter to her). "I always looked at music as a form of escape," she told *VH-1*. "You could be anything you wanted to be when you had music."

When Mariah was ten and eleven, she attended an arts camp in the summers. (Her mother had scraped up the money with the help of

R&B singer Minnie Riperton was a major influence on young Mariah. Riperton's multioctave vocal range was phenomenal, especially on her hit "Loving You." Riperton died from breast cancer in 1979, when she was thirty-one.

Mariah's childhood was not always a happy one, and she used music as a way to escape when things were too difficult. It wasn't long before her voice earned her praise and the reputation of a superstar in the making.

Mariah's father and other family members.) There, Mariah performed in *Fiddler on the Roof*, and she also played Maria in her school's production of *The Sound of Music*.

Mariah's voice was gaining her a reputation, and by the time she entered Greenlawn Junior High School on Long Island, she was certain she was destined to be a superstar singer. Her mother had finally managed to buy a house in a good neighborhood, so their life was more stable. School, however, was a constant struggle for Mariah.

She loved classes where she could use her creativity—writing and music were her strengths—but she was bored with everything else. She even forgot to take her eighth-grade finals. She told Rosie O'Donnell, "It's not that I deliberately did not take the finals. I always wanted to be prepared for tests, but I was always busy with my music."

At thirteen, Mariah was writing her own songs, mostly ballads and love songs that expressed her own life experiences. Her mother respected her talent and encouraged her to develop it. To help Mariah grow, Patricia enrolled her in acting workshops. When Mariah showed real talent, her mother took her to audition in New York City for roles in Broadway musicals. Mariah never actually landed a part, but the experience helped her to build self-confidence.

Despite her confidence in her musical abilities, however, Mariah suffered from plenty of other insecurities. She told *Seventeen* magazine:

> **"I always thought I was ugly. My best friend was this perfect-looking blonde, and there I was with all this frizzy hair and bushy eyebrows. I remember being in the seventh grade and really wanting to impress this guy, so I tried highlighting my hair but it came out all orange."**

Mariah's insecurity made her develop a "tough-girl" image at school. "For a while, I distanced myself from a lot of kids," she told *Dolly* magazine. "From the seventh grade on, I was the tough girl. I used to slam the cheerleaders into lockers and stuff like that. I wasn't really bad. I was just acting tough."

Meanwhile, musically, Mariah was growing up. Long Island recording studios sought her out as a **demo** singer for songwriters. Academically, though, she continued to struggle. Her constant absences from class earned her the nickname "Mirage," and her teachers and school administrators were worried about her. The vice principal later told *Newsday*:

> **"You could talk to her until you were blue in the face, and it didn't do any good. When you talked to her about it, she'd let you know it just wasn't that important in her life because she was going to be a rock star. She was fully convinced it was going to happen. Nothing was going to stand in her way."**

Mariah's mother insisted her daughter stay in school, but at the same time, she encouraged Mariah to pursue her musical career. As Mariah's recording career grew, it meant that Mariah commuted from Long Island to Manhattan after school to work all night with other musicians in a recording studio; she would get back home at three in the morning and have to be up four hours later to go to school. No wonder she was often late for her classes.

When Mariah was seventeen, she met Ben Margulies, another songwriter. He was seven years older than her, but they had a lot in common, and the two began a creative partnership. Ben told the *New York Times*:

> **"Mariah had the ability to just hear things in the air and to start developing songs out of them. Often, I would sit down and start playing something and from the feel of the chord, she would start singing melody lines and come up with a concept."**

By this time, school was definitely low on Mariah's priority list. Still, she managed to make it through her senior year and graduate from high school when she was seventeen. Shortly before her graduation, her mother remarried, leaving Mariah free to break away from her close bond with her mother. A week after her graduation, Mariah moved to New York City.

Making It on Her Own

Mariah's first year in the big city was a rough one. She worked a series of dead-end jobs and slept on a mattress in a tiny apartment. She had very few clothes, and she ate a lot of macaroni and cheese from a box.

"I had no money to buy a pair of shoes," she told *Jet*, "and so I would walk around in the snow in shoes that had holes in them."

After working all day, Mariah would get together with Ben and create songs all night. She was still convinced that success was just around the corner. Every few days, she would deliver another demo tape to one of New York's many record companies. She seldom got any further than the front desk—but she didn't give up.

Meanwhile, Mariah's older brother Morgan had also moved to New York City and was working as a doorman at a club. He was able to use his connections to persuade the club owner to book his sister for a series of performances on the club's slow nights. Mariah was nervous, and she wasn't a particularly smooth performer—but the opportunity meant she would have the chance to make more connections in the music world.

Eventually, those connections led to another opportunity for Mariah: in 1988, she became the backup singer for R&B singer Brenda K. Starr. Although Starr was far from being a famous artist herself, Mariah did have the chance to perform with her in a number of live shows, giving the music world more opportunities to hear her voice. Even better, Starr did what she could to help Mariah get her own career going. "She helped me out a lot," Mariah told *Ebony* magazine. "She was always saying, 'Here's my friend Mariah. Here's her tape. She sings. She writes.'"

Later that fall, Mariah received exciting news. Warner Brothers Records was offering her a solo recording contract with a $300,000 **advance**. However, the deal would take a while to go through. And in the meantime, Sony Records offered Mariah an even better deal.

Success was finally just around the corner.

The critics were right! Mariah's career was hot. Here, in this 1996 photo, Mariah shows off the American Music Awards she received for Best Pop-Rock Female Artist and Best Soul/R&B Female Artist. Many more awards were to come.

2

Success!

"**W**hen I heard and saw Mariah, there was absolutely no doubt that she was, in every way, destined for stardom," Tommy Mottola, the president of Sony Records, told the *New York Times*. Tommy was impressed with everything about Mariah: her voice, her songwriting, and her beauty. But as much as he liked her, he believed she needed to be shaped.

Stardom

Some things about being a star were wonderful, but some were hard to get used to. For instance, Mariah was used to working with Ben Margulies on her music. Together they had created the songs that had won her the contract with Sony, and she assumed they would produce her album together. Instead, she found that big-name producers like Rik Wake, Rhett Lawrence, and Narada Michael Walden were assigned to her album. These producers had worked with artists like Michael Jackson; Earth, Wind & Fire; and Smokey Robinson—but Mariah worried that her music would be turned into something that would sell rather than something that was true to her.

The songs Mariah had written were very personal. She told *Ebony* that "Vision of Love," one of the songs on the album, "represents everything in my life. It is a song from the heart." In another interview, this one with the *Chicago Tribune*, she said that a lot of the songs on the album "were written when I was kind of struggling. It was a harrowing emotional time in my life. [The songs] . . . were about things happening in my life." Mariah didn't want to lose that deep connection to her music. And she wasn't sure she wanted to be shaped into something that would sell—a star.

What's more, recording the album was exhausting. She flew back and forth across the country to studios in New York, Los Angeles, and San Rafael, California. Her long workdays often stretched far into the nights.

But the money that came with stardom helped compensate for some of the frustration. For the first time in her life, Mariah had all the money she needed—and then some. She bought herself a new Mustang convertible and lots of clothes.

And the executives at Sony Records, particularly Tommy Mottola, were more and more impressed with Mariah. Sony's marketing and publicity teams were determined to make her name a household word, and they carefully planned how her **debut** album, *Mariah Carey*, would be released. They budgeted $800,000 to produce the album—and a million dollars for promotion.

Finally, late in the spring of 1990, the album was ready to be released. She and Ben had created six of the album's ten songs, including "Vision of Love" and "Love Takes Time." For the first time, Mariah also **collaborated** with other musicians; she wrote "There's Got to Be a Way" with Rik Wake and "I Don't Wanna Cry" with Rhett Lawrence.

Sony had decided that "Vision of Love" would be the album's first single, and a video was shot for the song. Sony executives were not happy with the first video, so they reshot it; they wanted to convey an image of Mariah as a sultry new star.

Romance

When Tommy Mottola agreed to reshoot Mariah's video, at considerable expense to the company, rumors began to circulate about the special treatment he was giving Mariah. People said the record executive had fallen in love with the young singer.

Although the couple did not go public, the rumors were true. "Our relationship was kind of a different thing," Mariah told *Vibe* in 1996.

Sony Record executive Tommy Mottola (seen in this photo from 2005) took the young Mariah under his wing and guided her to early recording success. He was quite taken with Mariah's music—and with Mariah.

Though her fans couldn't tell, Mariah struggled with stage fright, and she didn't feel comfortable on stage and dreaded the thought of touring. But she worked through it, and her fans can always count on a good show.

"There was definitely some kind of chemistry going that was really intense." Despite the chemistry, however, Mottola knew he had to keep the relationship a secret. He was already in the midst of an ugly divorce, and he did not want scandal to hurt Mariah's entrance as a new star.

Fame

While some aspects of Mariah's life had to be kept quiet, in other ways she was constantly on display for the public. Early in June 1990, she appeared on the late-night shows, including the *Arsenio Hall Show* and the *Tonight Show*. Later, she sang "America the Beautiful" at game one of the NBA finals.

Meanwhile, "Vision of Love" was singing from radios across America, and by June 2, it had already entered *Billboard* magazine's top-100 list. By the time the entire album was released later that month, it was already on *Billboard*'s charts. By August, the single was number one, a position it would hold for four weeks. The album eventually was number one as well—and it stayed there for an incredible twenty-two weeks. *Mariah Carey* quickly went **platinum**.

Mariah was already working on her next album, and Mottola didn't want to push her too hard. She was not comfortable on stage, and he didn't want anything to hurt the reputation her songs were gaining. He did agree, however, to have Mariah perform at one live performance, the outdoor Summer Jam concert in California.

For Mariah, learning to deal with her stage fright was a constant struggle. Years later, she told *USA Today*:

> **❝Touring is hard for me because I'm not a ham. You have to be dynamic and showy and that's not second nature to me. I didn't get a chance to work my way up from the clubs, so performing is still pretty scary.❞**

Dealing with critical reviewers was another challenge that came along with fame. Some critics dismissed Mariah as a white girl trying to **exploit** black music. They didn't realize that Mariah's heritage meant she knew something of what it was like to grow up black.

Mariah kept going. In October 1990, she made another television appearance, this time on *Saturday Night Live*. Meanwhile, another single from her album was released, "Love Takes Time," and by November, it too had climbed to number one on the charts.

Awards

When the Grammy nominations were released, Mariah found herself nominated in five different categories:

- Best Pop Vocal Performance—Female
- Best New Artist
- Album of the Year
- Song of the Year
- Best Album

Mariah performed on the televised 1991 Grammy Awards. More than twenty million people around the world now knew who Mariah Carey was! Later in the evening, she went home with the awards for Best New Artist and Best Pop Vocal Performance—Female.

The awards and recognitions just kept coming. *Rolling Stone* recognized Mariah as Best New Female Singer in its annual readers' poll. Soul Train gave her Best New Artist, Best New Single, and Best New Album. Meanwhile, another single, "Someday," was released and quickly became her third number-one hit. "I Don't Wanna Cry" followed suit in the spring of 1991.

Emotions

While all this was happening, Mariah was also working on her second album, *Emotions.* "I didn't want this album to be someone else's vision of me," she told *USA Today.* "This time, I really collaborated. There's more of me on this album, and I let myself go a lot more." The album was an **homage** to Motown. The sounds of soul and gospel music rang in its songs.

The title song off the album was released at the end of August 1991, and it hit the *Billboard* top-100 charts immediately. Once the entire album was released, it slowly climbed to number one. By the end of the year, the album had sold three million copies. Some critics, however, pointed out that the album had failed to match her first album's success, and they criticized Mariah for going in such a different musical direction on her second album.

Mariah was happy, though. She had finally achieved what she had always dreamed. On top of that, Tommy Mottola's divorce had finally become official, and the couple was free to reveal their relationship to the world.

Going Live

Mariah was still nervous about touring—but her critics were starting to say she was purely a studio creation, that her talent wouldn't hold up to a live concert. Finally, she agreed to an MTV *Unplugged* concert that would only be thirty minutes long, in front of a relatively small audience.

The concert was so successful that MTV aired it over and over—and in June 1992, Sony decided to release a new album: *Mariah Carey:*

Mariah's 1991 album *Emotions* honored Motown. According to Mariah, this album reflected more of who she really was than did her first. Though it sold three million copies, it hadn't matched the success of her debut album.

MTV Unplugged. The album immediately shot to number three on the charts and in only a few months, sold more than two million copies.

This success was so unexpected that Mariah felt the money was more than she deserved or needed. She insisted that a portion of the sales from the album be given to a variety of charities.

Songwriter and Producer

Mariah's career was taking off in all directions. She helped Trey Lorenz produce his debut album and wrote two of the songs for him. Then she went on to write a song for Daryl Hall, "Help Me Find a Way to Your Heart." As the years went by, she would become a much-sought-after songwriter and producer for a number of artists, including Allure, 7 Mile, and Blaque.

Marriage and Music

But the biggest event of 1992 for Mariah was her engagement to Tommy Mottola in December. They planned a traditional—but extremely lavish—wedding for the following June. Mariah's custom-made gown, with its twenty-seven-foot train and ten-foot veil, cost somewhere around $25,000, while her designer shoes cost $1,000. On the guest list were all the big names from the entertainment industry, everyone from Barbra Streisand to Ozzy Osbourne, Billy Joel to Dick Clark.

While Mariah planned her wedding, she kept busy musically as well. Her third album, *Music Box,* was in production. Included on it was "Hero," from the soundtrack for the Dustin Hoffman–Geena Davis movie *Hero.*

The elaborate June 1993 wedding (patterned after Princess Diana's wedding to Prince Charles) made Tommy Mottola and Mariah Carey husband and wife. After a honeymoon in Hawaii, they were back at work in New York. The single "Dreamlover" came out in August, and *Music Box* was released in September. "Dreamlover" did well, holding its place as number one on the charts for eight weeks, but the album's climb to success was much slower. However, the album eventually made it to platinum.

Mariah's life seemed to be right on track. She conquered her fears of live performance and went on tour. Her marriage with Tommy seemed to be a success, and certainly her professional life was. The albums kept coming—a Christmas album in 1994, followed by

It wasn't long before Tommy Mottola and Mariah (seen in this 1995 photo) became more than mentor and up-and-coming star. They married in an elaborate ceremony in 1993. Unfortunately, the marriage that began with a storybook wedding didn't last; they divorced five years later.

Daydream in 1995, *Butterfly* in 1997, *#1s* in 1998, and *Rainbow* by 1999—and the awards followed right along after the albums. *Billboard* named her Female Artist of the Year in 1994; the next year, in 1995, she won the World Music Awards for World's Best-Selling Pop Artist, World's Best Recording Artist, and World's Overall Best-Performing Artist, as well as the American Music Awards for Favorite Pop/Rock Female Artist. She was nominated for six Grammy Awards, and she

Mariah had a big 1994. She was named *Billboard* Female Artist of the Year; she founded Camp Mariah; and she released her first Christmas album. Here, Mariah is ready to sign copies of her Christmas album for fans at a record store.

performed live at the televised Grammy ceremony with Boyz II Men. (To her great disappointment, however, she did not go home with a single award.)

The year 1996, brought Mariah more awards, including *Billboard*'s Special Award for Chart Performance, Hot 100 Singles Artist of the Year, Hot 100 Airplay Award, and Hot Adult Contemporary Artist of the Year. The same year, she won the World Music Award for World's Best-Selling R&B Female Artist of the Year, World's Best-Selling Pop Artist of the Year, World's Best-Selling American Female Artist of the Year, and World's Best-Selling Overall Recording Female Artist of the Year. In 1996, she also won BMI's Song of the Year and the American Music Awards' Favorite Pop/Rock Female Artist and Favorite Soul/R&B Female Artist. The year 1998 brought her another slew of awards, including the Aretha Franklin Award for Entertainer of the Year and the Soul Train Lady of Soul Award.

Best-Selling Female Artist of the Millennium

By the end of the twentieth century, Mariah Carey was the best-selling female artist of the millennium, with more weeks at the top of *Billboard*'s Hot 100 singles list than the Beatles. She had written the soundtracks for two major movies, *Men in Black* and *How the Grinch Stole Christmas*, and she had launched an acting career as well, starring in the semi-autobiographical movie *All That Glitters*, as well as landing a role in *Wise Girls* with Mira Sorvino. She was working with some of hip-hop's biggest names, including Missy Elliot, Wish Bone and Krazie Bone, Q-Tip, Dru Hill, and Sean "Puffy" Combs. To top all that, she had left Sony records and made an $80 million deal with Virgin Records (the biggest record contract ever).

But the final years of the twentieth century were not always easy for Mariah Carey. She faced a series of ups and downs, particularly when it came to the relationships in her life.

Mariah's star had risen so fast, perhaps too fast. Although there were still happy times, like being out with her dog in New York City, the road was about to get rocky, personally and professionally.

3

Troubles

ariah had achieved so much, so fast. The frantic pace of her professional life, however, was bound to put stress on her personal relationships. That kind of hectic schedule brings emotional stress as well. From all appearances, Mariah had made it to the top—but then her life took a nosedive.

Family Problems

While Mariah's life was going full-speed ahead, things had not gone so well for her sister Allison. She had become a mother, married, and divorced, all before she was twenty, and from there her life had gone into a downward spiral, with drugs and prostitution playing a major role in her self-destruction. Then Mariah found out her sister had AIDS.

Mariah put her career on hold while she helped her mother support Allison. Mariah and Patricia tried to persuade Allison to enter a drug-treatment program, where she would also receive AIDS counseling and treatment. Allison refused. Mariah and Patricia then brought Allison's son to live with Patricia. Allison was furious, and she severed all contact with her superstar sister. A few years later, however, she resurfaced with ugly accusations to the media about Mariah, as well as legal threats to her little sister.

While Mariah was coping with the rumors about her and her sister, plenty of other rumors about her were making the rounds as well.

Marriage Problems

Mariah married a much older man, who saw himself as far more experienced professionally than his wife. From the start, Tommy Mottola had sought to control all aspects of her career. As Mariah grew older and gained self-confidence, she naturally resented her husband calling all the shots. Rumors began to circulate in the media that Tommy Mottola viewed his wife as his very own creation, a puppet whose strings he could pull whenever he wanted.

Meanwhile, Mariah wanted to grow musically—and she wanted to try out some new directions in her upcoming album, *Daydream*. Connecting with her black heritage excited and inspired her—but Tommy Mottola saw things differently. When Mariah began working with rapper **mogul** Sean "Puffy" Combs and Ol' Dirty Bastard of the **gangsta rap** group Wu-Tan Clan, Tommy cringed at the idea of mixing Mariah's smooth pop ballads with what he viewed as "street music."

Mariah, however, had loved hip-hop music since she was a kid, and she believed in hip-hop's integrity and **validity** as a music form. She told *VH1*:

> **"The minute we heard the Sugar Hill Gang on the radio as kids, we started memorizing it. Hip-hop is an art form that continues to evolve. Music executives would say to me, 'This is a fad,' I'd be like, 'You don't even know what you're talking about. You guys are the last ones to know sometimes. I've been listening to this music since I was in fifth grade!"**

Hip-hop had been born in the 1970s in New York City's ghettos, springing up out of African American youths' frustration and anger in the face of poverty and prejudice. Mariah knew all about poverty and prejudice, and she loved hip-hop's pounding rhythms.

But Tommy Mottola felt very differently about the urban music—and he didn't trust the rappers she was hanging out with. Rumors were printed in magazines like *Stern, Star,* and *Vanity Fair* that Tommy had hired bodyguards to follow Mariah; that he listened in on her telephone calls; and that he was obsessed with the fear that Mariah would be caught in the middle of a rapper shoot-out.

Mariah had been a hip-hop fan since childhood, and she was excited at the possibility of working with rap legend and mogul Sean "Puffy" Combs. In 2005, they reunited at the release party for Mariah's *Emancipation of Mimi*.

By December 1996, Mariah had enough. She moved out of the mansion she shared with Tommy. A quick trip to the Dominican Republic in 1998 made their divorce official. In the meantime, Mariah had begun dating.

Romantic Ups and Downs

Mariah met Yankee shortstop Derek Jeter at a charity function, and she soon discovered they had a lot in common. Like Mariah, Derek came from a biracial family, and both understood what it meant to be a celebrity. The media went crazy with rumors about their relationship. In the midst of all the attention, their relationship failed to survive, and by mid-1998, they had broken up.

By the end of the year, Mariah had a new boyfriend, Latino singer Luis Miguel. In numerous interviews, she insisted that this time it was the real thing; she was really and truly in love. Their romance lasted three years—and then it too petered out.

Professional Struggles

Things had been going so well professionally in the 1990s—but as the new century began, her career began to wobble. At the same time that Mariah was dealing with so much personally, she also faced harsh criticism from reviewers. Her acting in *Glitter* was said to be dull and unprofessional, and the soundtrack from the film met with the same lack of enthusiasm. *Rolling Stone* said *Glitter* had "zero melodic or emotional punch," and other reviews were just as critical if not more so. With so much negative attention, it's not surprising that the album failed to make much money.

After *Glitter* fell flat, Virgin Records decided they wanted out of their deal with Mariah. They had already paid her $21 million, but now they bought out the rest of the contract for $28 million. More bad publicity for Mariah followed.

Emotional Breakdown

With everything she was going through, it's no wonder that Mariah fell apart emotionally. She told *VH1*, "I'm honestly, really delirious and stressed out and overworked and doing too much. . . . It's an insane time in my life. Everything is going really fast." In an interview with *Parade* magazine, she said, "One day, I looked around and thought, 'Why did I ever expect that if I had this success, I would have happiness too?'"

After her divorce, Mariah thought she found true love with Latino singer Luis Miguel, and in this photo from 2001, they do look like a happy couple. But after dating for three years, the couple broke up.

Happiness was definitely slipping through Mariah's Carey's fingers. As if everything else Mariah was facing wasn't enough, her father died of cancer the same year that Virgin backed out of its contract, the same year that her romance with Luis Miguel ended. Mariah couldn't sleep, couldn't eat, but she couldn't stop working either.

New rumors were traveling through the media now: Mariah Carey was falling apart at a very personal level. Rambling, suicidal messages to her fans started appearing on her Web site. For her appearance on MTV's *Total Request Live*, she showed up dressed only in a T-shirt; then she did an impromptu striptease and handed out Popsicles to

When things started falling apart for Mariah, everything seemed to happen at once. Her marriage and relationships failed; her film was panned, and the film soundtrack didn't sell; Virgin bought out her record-setting contract; and her father died. Even the strongest would have difficulty coping.

the teenage audience. By the end of July 2001, she had checked into a psychiatric hospital. Her **publicist** announced that she was taking a break from all her public appearances. Another hospitalization, reportedly for exhaustion, followed later that year.

Somehow, though, Mariah found the strength to endure. In an interview with *Parade*, she said that a memory from her childhood gave her strength:

> **"It was when I was four years old. My parents' battles, craziness—whatever—was going on in my house. Everybody was crying. It got to the point where the police were called. That's how intense it was. Then someone called Nana Reese [her father's aunt, a Pentecostal minister] to come to the house, because we needed her. . . . Nana was the real thing, a healer. She laid her hands on me, and I felt in that moment a connection between us. She said, 'You're going to be OK. All your dreams are going to come true.' The faith Nana Reese and my mother had in me carried me through. And because I know I'm not perfect, I've had to learn forgiveness. I try wholeheartedly to forgive anyone I feel has wronged me, because I hope people who feel I've wronged them will forgive me. I want to be a forgiving person."**

Mariah forgave herself for all the disasters that had taken place in her professional and personal life. And then she went back to doing what she had always done best—making music.

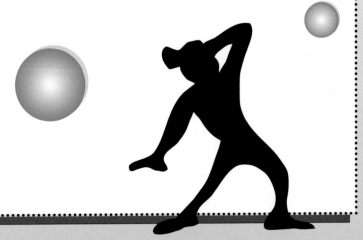

Critics and some record executives were ready to write off Mariah as just another has-been, whose star had crashed as quickly as it had risen. The only thing was, they forgot to ask Mariah, who definitely had other ideas!

4

Return of the Voice

People said Mariah Carey's star had set for good. They predicted that her career was over. They said she had used up all her musical ability. Some critics even referred to her incredibly high notes as "dog whistles" that lacked any depth or meaning. But Mariah ignored the critics. She picked herself up and proved them all wrong.

The Emancipation of Mimi

Mariah's ninth studio album, released in 2005, demonstrated that she still has what it takes when it comes to music. It became the year's best-selling album, and its second single, "We Belong Together," became the biggest hit of the year, topping the charts for fourteen weeks. Another single from the album, "Don't Forget About Us," became Mariah's seventeenth song to top the *Billboard* charts, tying her with Elvis Presley for the most number-one songs by a solo artist. (Only the Beatles, who had twenty-one number-one songs, had more.)

On Mariah's Web site, she explains the inspiration behind *The Emancipation of Mimi*:

> **"With this album, I am embracing my independence and celebrating the person that I have become. Over the years, I have evolved into a better person and an even better artist. For the first time in my life, I am proud and unafraid to be who I really am, and that's what the music of this album and its title reflect. By ... referencing 'Mimi,' a nickname used only by those closest to me, I am inviting my fans into my life."**

Mariah's voice continues to be incredible. She's credited with influencing other singers such as Christina Aguilera and Kelly Clarkson. Both MTV and *Blender* magazine voted her voice at the top of their list of music's greatest voices. The *Guinness Book of World Records*, in its 2003 edition, credited Mariah with the record for the highest note hit by a human (a note once considered to be beyond the human range). Mariah also holds the record for the largest vocal range.

Mariah's talents continue to earn her more official recognition. In 2002, she won *Billboard*'s Top R&B/Hip-Hop Single for "Loverboy." The next year, as she regained her stride professionally and personally, she won an impressive line-up of awards:

- the Quincy Jones Award for Outstanding Career

- Soul Train Music Award for Achievements in the Field of Entertainment—Female

- World Music Diamond Award for over 100 million album sales worldwide

- RIAA Certification Award for more than a hundred **gold**, platinum, and multiplatinum certificates

- MTV's Free Ride Award for Best Vehicle Hook-Up in "Loverboy"

- Sweden's NRJ Radio Music Award for Most Played Artist (1993–2003)

In 2005, Mariah made a comeback that astounded everyone, except perhaps Mariah herself. _The Emancipation of Mimi_ became the year's best-selling album. Here, Frank Briegmann of Universal presents Mariah with the Gold Award for the album.

The year 2004 brought Mariah another handful of awards—but 2005 was truly an incredible year for the singer critics had once dismissed as a "has-been." The list goes on and on:

- MTV Japan Video Music Award for International Video Icon

- Capital Award for Outstanding Contribution to Music

2003年
JUL. **7**

希望下半月

HOPE

封面人物 玛丽亚·凯莉
半月刊
2003年7月15日出版
定价￥10元
涉外价US$4

很难不美丽
男女同厠

松糕鞋又复辟了
高级定做时装解密

凌怪

妇检白皮书

特别策划 粉爱三毛

In Love With Echo

Mariah's talents, her record-holding vocal range, and the reclaiming of her spot in the music world were appreciated all over the world. She even appeared on the cover of the July 2003 issue of *Hope*, a Chinese magazine.

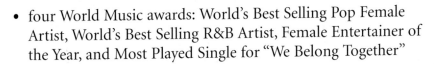

- four World Music awards: World's Best Selling Pop Female Artist, World's Best Selling R&B Artist, Female Entertainer of the Year, and Most Played Single for "We Belong Together"

- two Teen Choice awards for Choice Music: R&B Artist and Choice Love Song for "We Belong Together"

- two Lady of Soul awards for Best R&B/Soul Album, Solo (*The Emancipation of Mimi*) and Best R&B/Soul Single, Solo ("We Belong Together")

- the United Kingdom's Kiss Award for Best Female Artist

- four VIBE awards: Artist of the Year, Album of the Year (*The Emancipation of Mimi*), Best R&B Song ("We Belong Together"), and R&B Voice of the Year

- American Music Award for Favorite Soul/R&B Female Artist

- Germany's Bambi Award for Pop International Artist

- five Billboard Music awards: Female Billboard 200 Album Artist of the Year, Female R&B/Hip-Hop Artist of the Year, Hot 100 Song of the Year ("We Belong Together"), Hot 100 Airplay of the Year ("We Belong Together"), and Rhythmic Top 40 Title of the Year ("We Belong Together")

- four Radio Music awards: Artist of the Year—Urban and Rhythmic Radio, Song of the Year—Mainstream Hit Radio ("We Belong Together"), Song of the Year—Urban and Rhythmic Radio ("We Belong Together"), and Radio Legend Award

When 2006 came along, Mariah more than demonstrated that she was definitely the "Comeback Kid." At the 2006 Grammys, she won three awards: Best Contemporary R&B Award for *The Emancipation of Mimi*, Best R&B Song for "We Belong Together," and Best Female R&B Performance for "We Belong Together." She also won six Groosevelt Music Awards:

- Album of the Year for *The Emancipation of Mimi*

- Song of the Year for "We Belong Together"

In 2004, Mariah was honored by the Female First Awards, Groovevolt Music Awards, and MTV Asia Awards. And, she got to meet "the Mouse"! Here, Mariah poses with Mickey Mouse before taking part in the annual Walt Disney World Christmas Day Parade.

With *The Emancipation of Mimi*, Mariah was undoubtedly back on top of the music scene. But, her true fans had never doubted for a single minute that she would be. In this 2005 photo, Mariah signs autographs and meets some enthusiastic fans in London.

- Best Pop Female Album for *The Emancipation of Mimi*

- Best Pop Female Song Performance for "We Belong Together"

- Best Pop Unreleased Album Track for *Circles*

- Best R&B/Soul Female Song Performance for "We Belong Together"

The Emancipation of Mimi returned Mariah to the Grammy winners' circle in 2006 for the first time since 1991. Nominated for eight awards, she took home three. Unfortunately, all of them came before the televised show.

And Mariah wasn't done. In 2006, she also won:

- four Jammy awards for Best Female Vocalist, Best Slow Jam ("We Belong Together"), Best CD/Album (*The Emancipation of Mimi*), and Best Song ("We Belong Together")

- the TRL awards for First Lady of TRL and Retired Videos Award ("We Belong Together," "Shake It Off," and "Don't Forget About Us")

- the Soul Train awards for Best-Female Album (*The Emancipation of Mimi*) and Best-Female Single ("We Belong Together")

Mariah had become a bridge between hip-hop and pop. She had also proved that both she and hip-hop had staying power.

But over the years, Mariah has proved something else as well—that she is a person who uses her talent to do good.

Mariah has a huge heart to go along with her huge talent. Many of her good works bring happiness to children, at least for a little while. Among her projects is an annual Thanksgiving dinner for inner-city children sponsored by Mariah's Fresh Air Fund.

5

Doing Good

Some of Mariah Carey's awards have been received for something besides her talent. For example, in 2003, she won both the Z100 Award for her musical and **philanthropic** contributions to the New York City area and the Fresh Air Fund's Salute to American Heroes. In 2006, she also won the **NAACP**'s award for her contributions on behalf of black Americans.

Making a Difference

Back in the 1990s, as Mariah gained her independence from Tommy Motolla's influence, she knew she wanted to use both her talent and her wealth to help others. In 1999, she sang a duet with famous tenor Luciano Pavarotti to benefit Kosovo refugees and Guatemalan post–civil war victims. She also did what she could to help the National Multiple Sclerosis Foundation.

But even as early as 1994, Mariah was doing what she could to reach out to those in need.

Camp Mariah

Mariah Carey helped found Camp Mariah in 1994 as part of the Fresh Air Fund's Career Awareness Program, which focuses on expanding the educational and career options for New York City's adolescents. Today the camp provides three-and-a-half-week summer camp sessions for nearly three hundred boys and girls. The program introduces young people to specific career fields—science and technology, communications, and health and fitness—but the kids get to enjoy traditional camping activities as well, such as hiking, swimming, and singing around campfires. Campers also attend classes and workshops in creative writing, journalism, photography, television and video production, fashion design, dance, computer applications, and more.

Mariah makes regular appearances at the camp. She often brings along her music-industry friends to inspire the campers and prove to them that no dream is impossible. Sometimes, she takes the kids out for a day and brings them along to whatever project she's currently working on.

Make-A-Wish Foundation

The Make-A-Wish Foundation grants the wishes of children and young adults with life-threatening illnesses. Mariah has been impressed with this organization and with the young people who have battled so much. In January 2000, she gave up her seats at the 27th Annual American Music Awards to two young people from the Make-A-Wish Foundation, and she dedicated her Lifetime Achievement Award to the two girls. She later took them with her for a *Rolling Stone* magazine photo shoot. Later that year, she met backstage after her performance at Wembley Arena with a Make-A-Wish Foundation teen who had fought Hodgkin's lymphoma. Also later that year, Mariah was presented with the Make-A-Wish Foundation's award for being the Celebrity Wish Granter of the Year. In October 2001, Mariah donated $100,000 to the Make-A-Wish Foundation, but Mariah wanted to do more than just give money—so she brought two Make-A-Wish youngsters to the **premiere** of *Glitter*.

Save The Music Foundation

VH1's Save The Music Foundation has two primary missions: to restore music education programs in America's public schools; and to raise awareness of the positive impact music participation has on students. Over the years, Mariah has done what she can to help.

On April 17, 2005, she took part in a benefit concert for Save The Music, with three performances, including the show opener, "It's Like That" with Jermaine Dupri and Fat Man Scoop, followed by "With You

Keeping music in the schools is important to Mariah, and she participates in VH1's Save The Music program. In 2001, she spoke to New Jersey students as part of that program. Former president Bill Clinton (left) also lent his support to the program.

I'm Born Again" with John Legend, and then closing the show with "I'll Be There" with Trey Lorenz. "I've been involved with Save the Music for a while," Mariah said at the concert. "It is important because they do tend, when they're cutting costs, to take away some of the programs that help kids develop their creativity."

The National Adoption Center

The National Adoption Center expands opportunities for children throughout the United States, particularly for children with special needs and those from minority cultures. Mariah has been involved with this organization since 1998, when she attended the Adoption Fair at New York's City Hall Park with Mayor Rudolph Giuliani to discuss foster care and adoption. The following year, she filmed a public service announcement for the New York City local chapter of the National Adoption Center, and on the February 8, 2000, airing of the *Rosie O'Donnell Show*, Mariah announced that retail sales of her "Thank God I Found You" single would be donated to the National Adoption Center. The same month, she held a charity luncheon at a New York restaurant, where she brought in kids from the local chapter of the National Adoption Center. She had presents for all the children and even brought in several of her dogs, so the children could play with them. On December 18, 2000, she took a hundred children from the National Adoption Center for a pre-Christmas retreat at her rented home in Aspen, Colorado. Alongside Mariah, the children went sledding, made gingerbread houses, sang songs, and chatted with one of their favorite singers. A year later, Mariah hosted and performed on the CBS *Home for the Holidays*, which was aimed at helping to build a positive image of adoption and the children who wait for homes. Mariah spent Thanksgiving 2002 in Tokyo, Japan, with fifteen children from Seibi Home, a Japanese foster care house that hosts 160 children.

When Barbara Walters asked Mariah why so much of her charity work deals with children and adoption, Mariah answered, "There's over 500,000 kids in the system who need permanent homes and families and a lot of times in our daily life we don't think about things like that. All children need to be loved."

Police Athletic League

The Police Athletic League offers personal guidance to youth and provides recreational activities, as well as opportunities in performing

Mariah takes her concern for children all over the world. While in Japan on a promo tour in 2002, she invited fifteen children from a foster-care home there to join her for a real Thanksgiving dinner.

and creative arts. In the very beginning of her career, Mariah became involved with this organization when she attended a dinner ceremony benefiting the cause in 1991. The following year, she sang Christmas carols at a children's Christmas party sponsored by New York's Police Athletic League. In 1994, she made several trips to local New York–based chapters of the Police Athletic League to speak with children in the after-school programs. Mariah—who says she hates playing sports—even took time to play basketball with the kids.

Other Good Causes

Mariah has also taken part in numerous other good causes, including the "United We Stand" benefit concert after the September 11, 2001, terrorist attacks on New York City and Washington, D.C. She has

Mariah recognizes the importance of reading and of books to children. In 2005, she took time out of her busy schedule to read a selection from *Peter Pan* to one hundred children at a holiday celebration.

worked on behalf of such causes as AIDS research and the Vote or Die! campaign started by P. Diddy (who used to be known as Sean "Puffy" Combs). Mariah also donates her time on behalf of Mexican children with handicaps.

What Mariah Loves

On many Web sites Mariah is quoted as saying:

> **"Music is what I love and it's what I feel and it's in me and to know that I can do something that I enjoy and hopefully bring some enjoyment to other people through what I do is an incredible feeling and I'm just really thankful for it."**

Clearly, Mariah has come a long way—and her passion for her music is clear. Whatever she's doing, whether singing, songwriting, or simply sharing her time with those less fortunate, Mariah's message can be summarized with her words at a 1995 Madison Square Garden concert: "Don't ever give up! Never ever listen to anyone, when they try to discourage you!"

Mariah Carey could have been discouraged as a young girl, tagging along after her single-parent mother. She might have given up when she was seventeen, during that first hard year in New York City. And certainly, no one would have blamed her if she had just quietly retired after her public breakdown in 2001. But Mariah Carey doesn't give up—and the world is better because of her.

1970s Hip-hop is born in New York City ghettoes.

1970 Mariah Carey is born on March 27.

1973 Her parents divorce.

1988 Mariah becomes a backup singer for Brenda K. Starr.

1990 Her debut album, *Mariah Carey*, is released.

"Vision of Love" makes the *Billboard* top-100 list and hits number one.

1991 She receives two Grammy awards and performs on the television broadcast.

She receives awards from *Rolling Stone* and Soul Train.

Her second album, *Emotions*, is released as an homage to Motown.

Mariah becomes involved with the Police Athletic League in New York City.

1992 Releases *Mariah Carey: MTV Unplugged* and donates a portion of the profits to charity.

1993 Marries Tommy Mottola.

1994 *Billboard* names her Female Artist of the Year.

Founds Camp Mariah.

1995 Wins three World Music Awards, an American Music Award, and is nominated for six Grammys.

1996 Wins three *Billboard* awards, four World Music Awards, a BMI award, and two American Music Awards.

Leaves husband Tony Mottola.

1998 Wins the Aretha Franklin Award for Entertainer of the Year and the Soul Train Lady of Soul Award.

Divorces Tony Mottola.

Participates in the Adoption Fair on behalf of the National Adoption Center.

1999 Performs with Luciano Pavarotti in a benefit for Kosovo refugees and Guatemalan post–civil war victims.

2000 Receives the Make-A-Wish Foundation's award for Celebrity Wish Granter of the Year.

Announces that retail sales of the single "Thank God I Found You" will be donated to the National Adoption Center.

Takes 100 children from the National Adoption Center on a pre-Christmas vacation to Aspen.

2001 Checks into a psychiatric hospital.

Participates in the "United We Stand" benefit concert.

2002 Wins *Billboard* award.

Visits a foster-care house in Tokyo, Japan.

2003 *Guinness Book of World Records* credits Mariah with the record for the highest note ever hit by a human voice.

Wins the Z100 Award for musical and philanthropic contributions to the New York City area.

2005 *The Emancipation of Mimi* becomes the year's best-selling album; it's "Don't Forget About Us" is her seventeenth number-one song, tying the record for number-one songs by a solo artist.

The Emancipation of Mimi wins numerous awards.

Participates in a benefit concert for Save The Music.

Performs at Live 8.

2006 Wins three Grammys and six Groosevolt Music Awards, among others.

Wins an award from the NAACP for her contributions on behalf of black Americans.

Embarks on The Adventures of Mimi tour.

2007 Is inducted into the Long Island Music Hall of Fame.

It is announced that Mariah is the new "face" of Pinko, an Italian fashion line.

Receives a star on the Hollywood Walk of Fame.

Discography

Solo Albums

1990	*Mariah Carey*	1998	*#1s*
1991	*Emotions*	1999	*Rainbow*
1992	*MTV Unplugged*	2001	*Glitter*
1993	*Music Box*		*Greatest Hits*
1994	*Merry Christmas*	2002	*Charmbracelet*
1995	*Daydream*	2003	*The Remixes*
1997	*Butterfly*	2005	*The Emancipation of Mimi*

Number-one Singles

1990	"Vision of Love"
	"Love Takes Time"
1991	"Someday"
	"I Don't Wanna Cry"
	"Emotions"
1992	"I'll Be There"
	(with Trey Lorenz)
1993	"Dreamlover"
	"Hero"
1995	"Fantasy"

	"One Sweet Day"
	(with Boyz II Men)
1996	"Always Be My Baby"
1997	"Honey"
1998	"My All"
1999	"Heartbreaker" (with Jay-Z)
2000	"Thank God I Found You"
	(with Joe and 98 Degrees)
2005	"We Belong Together"
	"Don't Forget About Us"

Selected Television Appearances

1998	*Mariah Carey: Around the World*
1999	*Mariah Carey's Homecoming Special*
2000	*VH1 Divas 2000: A Tribute to Diana Ross; The Rosie O'Donnell Show*
2001	*The E! True Hollywood Story*
2002	*Ally McBeal; Fame Academy; Children in Need*
2003	*I Love the '80s Strikes Back;*

	Intimate Portrait: Mariah Carey; The Proud Family
2005	*Gottschalk & Friends; Tickled Pink; Uncut Mariah Carey; Cribs; Late Night with David Letterman; The Tonight Show with Jay Leno; The Ellen DeGeneres Show; The Oprah Winfrey Show*
2006	*The Tyra Banks Show*

Film

1999	*The Bachelor*
2001	*Glitter*
2002	*WiseGirls*
2005	*State Property 2*
	The Sweet Science
2007	*Tennessee*

Video

1991	*Mariah #1's*
2000	*Bone Thugs-N-Harmony: Greatest Video Hits*
2001	*Babyface: A Collection of Hit Videos*
2002	*Behind the Scenes of WiseGirls*

Selected Awards

1990   BMI Songwriters Award; Soul Train Music Awards

1991   American Music Award; Billboard Music Awards; Grammy Awards

1992   Billboard Music Awards; BMI Pop Award

1993   American Music Award

1994   American Music Award; Billboard Music Award; Bravo Magazine Award; MTV Europe Music Award; Smash Hits Award

1995   American Music Awards; Archer Awards; World Music Awards

1996   Billboard Music Awards; Gold Disc Awards; National Dance Music Award; World Music Awards

1997   VH1 Award

1998   American Music Award; International Achievement in Arts Award; Soul Train Lady of Soul Awards

1999   Billboard Music Award; Broadcast Film Critics Association Award; Congressional Award Foundation: Howard Humanitarian Award; Horizon Award; NAACP Image Award; Academy Award

2000   American Music Award; VH1 Awards; DMX Awards

2001   Make-A-Wish Foundation's 2000 Chris Grecius Award; Radio Music Award

2002   Billboard Music Awards

2003   Soul Train Awards; The Fresh Air Fund's Salute to American Heroes Award; World Music Award

2004   Female First Awards; Groovevolt Music Awards; MTV Asia Award

2005   American Music Awards; Groovevolt Music Awards; Soul Train Lady of Soul Awards; Teen Choice Awards; Teen People Awards; Vibe Awards; XM Nation Music Award

2006   Grammy Awards; Groovevolt Music Awards; Jammy Awards; NAACP Award; Soul Train Awards

Books

Parker, Judy. *Mariah Carey*. New York: Franklin Watts, 2001.

Shapiro, Marc. *Mariah Carey: The Unauthorized Biography*. Toronto, Ont.: ECW Press, 2001.

Wellman, Sam. *Mariah Carey (Galaxy of Superstars)*. Philadelphia: Chelsea House Publishers, 2000.

Magazines

Chambers, Veronica. "Mariah on Fire." *Newsweek*, November 22, 1999.

Hoffman, Melody K. "Mariah Carey: On Her Past, Present & Future in Music." *Jet*, April 25, 2005.

Morgan, Joan. "Free at Last: Mariah Carey." *Essence*, April 1, 2005.

Norent, Lynn. "Mariah Carey: 'Not Another White Girl Trying to Sing Black.'" *Ebony*, March 1, 1991.

Web Sites

Fresh Air Fund
www.freshair.org

Make-A-Wish Foundation
www.makeawish.org

The Mariah Carey Archives
www.mcarchives.com

Mariah Carey official Web site
www.mariahcarey.com

Mariah Daily
www.mariahdaily.com

Police Athletic League
www.nationalpal.org

VH1 Save The Music
www.vh1savethemusic.com

advance—a payment made before it is due.

bigotry—intolerance toward people who hold different views, especially on matters of politics, religion, or ethnicity.

civil rights movement—organized efforts during the late 1950s and 1960s to gain the rights all citizens of a society deserve to have.

collaborated—worked together on something.

debut—the first time.

demo—a recorded sample of music produced for promotional purposes.

exploit—take advantage of.

gangsta rap—a type of rap music in which the lyrics tend to deal with gangs and violence.

gold—signifying that a record has sold 500,000 copies.

gospel—highly emotional evangelical vocal music that originated among African American Christians in the southern United States.

homage—a show of respect toward someone or something.

industrialized—adapted factory-based methods of production and manufacturing.

interracial—involving different races.

mogul—an important or powerful person.

NAACP—National Association for the Advancement of Colored People; an organization that advocates for the rights of people of color.

Pentecostal—belonging or relating to any Christian denomination that emphasizes the workings of the Holy Spirit, interprets the Bible literally, and adopts an informal demonstrative approach to religious worship.

philanthropic—showing kindness, charitable concern, and generosity toward other people.

platinum—music having sold one million copies as a single or two million as a record or CD.

premiere—the first public performance of a film.

prestigious—much admired and respected.

publicist—the person responsible for obtaining media publicity for a client.

R&B—rhythm and blues; a musical style combining elements of blues and jazz, originally developed by African American musicians.

segregated—purposely kept apart, usually based on race or religion.

soul—a style of African American music with a strong emotional quality, related to gospel music and rhythm and blues.

validity—justifiability, being well-grounded, meaningful, and worthy of significance.

Like Mariah Carey, **Celicia Scott**'s talents showed up early: Celicia has been a storyteller since she was three years old, and her first story was published when she was nineteen. Although Celicia confesses that she can't sing at all, she's enjoyed the chance to tell a singer's story.

Picture Credits